MARGRIET RUURS

Illustrated by W. ALLAN HANCOCK

AMAZING ANIMALS

THE REMARKABLE THINGS THAT CREATURES DO

 TUNDRA BOOKS

To Nico, always keep asking questions and searching for answers! – M.R.

To my parents, Allan and Joyce, for encouraging my interest in art, and to my wife, Taryn, and our children, Ezra and Sage, for filling my life with joy and inspiration. – W.A.H.

Text copyright © 2011 by Margriet Ruurs
Illustrations copyright © 2011 by W. Allan Hancock

Published in Canada by Tundra Books,
75 Sherbourne Street, Toronto, Ontario M5A 2P9

Published in the United States by Tundra Books of Northern New York,
P.O. Box 1030, Plattsburgh, New York 12901

Library of Congress Control Number: 2010928806

Library and Archives Canada Cataloguing in Publication

Ruurs, Margriet, 1952-
Amazing animals : the remarkable things that creatures
do / Margriet Ruurs ; illustrator, W. Allan Hancock.

ISBN 978-0-88776-973-3

1. Animal behavior–Juvenile literature. I. Hancock, W. Allan.
II. Title.

QL751.5.R89 2011   j591.5   C2010-903181-4

We acknowledge the financial support of the Government of Canada through the Book Publishing Industry Development Program (BPIDP) and that of the Government of Ontario through the Ontario Media Development Corporation's Ontario Book Initiative. We further acknowledge the support of the Canada Council for the Arts and the Ontario Arts Council for our publishing program.

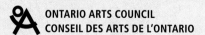

ONTARIO ARTS COUNCIL
CONSEIL DES ARTS DE L'ONTARIO

Medium: acrylic on masonite
Design by Andrew Roberts & W. Allan Hancock
Scans provided by Grant Kernan, AK Photos

Printed and bound in China

1 2 3 4 5 6   16 15 14 13 12 11

INTRODUCTION

What's the largest animal on Earth? Which bird is the fastest? How long do animals live? We share our planet with different species, many of which have existed much longer than humans. While researching this project, I came across astounding animal facts: Did you know that the earliest insect lived more than 350 million years ago? That's over 100 million years before the first dinosaurs! Did you know that a slug has three noses; an octopus has three hearts; and an earthworm has no eyes, no nose, no ears, and no lungs, but it has five hearts? I wrote *Amazing Animals* in the hope that it will urge you to research and explore the animal world for yourself, and that in the process, you, too, will be amazed at the information you find.

Some of the animals in this book are endangered. We must all do our part to protect them and keep them from becoming extinct. You can help by learning as much as you can about wildlife, joining an environmental organization, and respecting all species with which we share our planet.

Margriet

SIZE AND STRENGTH

Size and strength are just two of the many physical features that protect animals and enable them to find food, shelter, and mates. Physical features often adapt over many generations.

Native to Africa, the **ostrich** is the largest bird in the world. It stands about 2 meters (6.6 feet) tall and weighs approximately 154 kilograms (340 pounds). The ostrich starts life in the largest of all eggs – as big as a cantaloupe! The ostrich's strong, long legs are its main defense – they can deliver powerful kicks and run up to 70 kilometers (44 miles) per hour!

© W. Allan Hancock

Found in South America, the **green anaconda** is considered the largest and strongest snake in the world. With an average length of 8.8 meters (29.8 feet), it coils its powerful body around its prey, squeezing with incredible strength. With every breath its prey struggles to take, the snake's grip tightens. Then it eats and slowly digests its dinner.

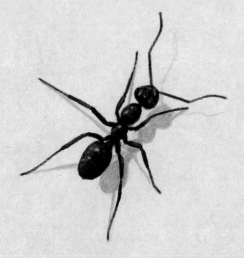

The **black ant** is so strong that it can carry ten to twenty times its own weight – that's about the same as you lifting a horse over your head! The black ant is one of the most abundant insect species on Earth. If you could put every insect in the world together on a scale, they would weigh more than all other animals combined.

The **blue whale** is the largest mammal to ever live – even bigger than the biggest dinosaur. It is found in the Antarctic, Pacific, and Atlantic oceans. While its average length is 25 meters (82 feet), the longest blue whale ever measured was over 33 meters (108 feet); that's almost as long as three school buses in a row! A blue whale can weigh up to 150 tons, and its heart alone weighs almost as much as a small car.

The **sturgeon** is one of the largest freshwater fish. It can grow 5 meters (16 feet) long! That's longer than many fishing boats. It can also live to a ripe old age – over a century!

The **giant Pacific octopus** is one of the largest of its species. Its arms can grow as long as 9 meters (30 feet), which is equivalent to the height of a three-storey building!

REPRODUCTION

Each animal species has its own specific way of producing offspring: through giving birth, by hatching eggs, or both. The survival of a species depends on its reproduction rate.

Emperor penguins live in Antarctica. Once a female lays her egg, she immediately transfers it to her mate. He will carry it on the top of his feet, covered by a thick fold of skin to protect it from the frigid -60ºC (-76ºF) weather. The female emperor penguin then returns to the open sea for food. While their mates are gone, males in the colony will huddle together for nine weeks, keeping the eggs warm and safe until they hatch. When the females return, their bellies are full with food to share with their young.

The **great white shark** is found along warm coastlines all across the world. It is ovoviviparous, which means its eggs grow and hatch inside of the shark, prompting the shark to give birth to live babies. The great white shark is born ready to hunt, so it doesn't need to be nursed. After it's born, the baby immediately swims away from its mother and into the world alone.

Native to Australia, **kangaroos** are the largest marsupials. Females carry their joeys in their pouches, where the babies stay until they are fully developed. Kangaroos can have three babies at different stages simultaneously: one in the womb, another in the pouch, and an older offspring that is out of the pouch and being weaned. When this happens, the fertilized egg growing inside of the female kangaroo will "pause" in its development until the joey matures and the fetus can take its place in the pouch.

© W. Allan Hancock

Did you know that **fig wasps** have a symbiotic relationship with fig trees? A fig wasp pollinates the flowers of the tree, which helps the tree produce its sweet fruit. In return, a female wasp lays her eggs inside the tree's fruit, where they stay until they hatch. But not all of the eggs survive, which means that some of the crunchy stuff inside of a fig cookie is the remains of wasps.

As the only survivor of a large group of reptiles that roamed the earth at the same time as dinosaurs, not much has changed for the **tuatara** during the last 225 million years. Native to New Zealand, the tuatara only produces eggs every two to five years, and its eggs take about two years to hatch. The gender of a baby tuatara depends on the temperature of the soil surrounding the egg: the warmer the temperature, the more likely the baby will be male. In fact, if the soil is just one degree above 21°C (70°F), a female embryo can change into a male.

COMMUNICATION

The different ways that animals communicate send out important messages to their own species and to others. A wagging tail, sniffing and baring teeth, or birdsong are just some of the ways animals communicate.

You'll find a **grouper** in the Atlantic Ocean, but beware – it is sneaky. A grouper uses its swim bladder to produce a loud, booming noise that scares away divers and other creatures that approach it.

Found in all of the world's oceans, **orcas** are often called whales, but they're really dolphins. Orcas use clicks as echolocation to navigate, and they use whistles and calls to communicate with each other. An orca's call can sound as loud as a jet plane's engine! Scientists think different orca pods may have their own unique dialects.

13

A native to New Guinea, the male **bird of paradise** likes to show off his colors. He can put on quite a show in the process: At times, he will perch on a branch, doing a dance. Other times, he will sweep leaves from the forest floor, creating his own stage – and with the sun shining down through the trees, he even has a spotlight! All this and trailing plumes, velvety feathers, a cape, quills, and dazzling colors help the male bird of paradise attract his mate.

The **western diamondback rattlesnake** lives in the southwestern United States. It sheds its skin two or three times a year, and some of that dried skin left behind forms its rattle. It shakes its rattle to communicate with other rattlesnakes (this is called caudaling), but it also shakes it as a warning when it feels threatened. When you hear this rattle – beware!

A **firefly** produces light from a chemical reaction called bioluminescence. Female fireflies use their lights to attract friends … and foes. Males from other insect species often mistake this as a mating call from one of their own. When a male from another insect species approaches a female firefly, she quickly gobbles him up before he realizes that he's been fooled!

HOMEBUILDING

From dens to burrows to hives, animal homes range from simple indentations in the grass to the most elaborate constructions. An animal's home is where it feels safe, where it sleeps, where it reproduces, and where it hibernates or estivates to escape extreme weather conditions.

The male **betta fish** lives in shallow, tropical waters and spends a lot of time making his bubble nest. He blows and gathers bubbles at the water surface, making sure there are enough to cushion the eggs that his mate will lay. When the female betta fish releases her eggs, he quickly collects them in the safety of the nest, standing guard until they hatch.

The North American **beaver** is an architect and engineer. It is second only to a human in its ability to change the environment. A beaver's teeth are self-sharpening and keep growing its entire life. They help them cut down trees as thick as a leg in just minutes, and it uses the felled trees to build dams. Dams can change the flow of rivers and create ponds and lakes. Beavers build their homes (also called lodges) in the ponds and lakes that they make. The largest dam ever found was in northern Alberta, and it measured 850 meters (2,789 feet) long.

The **weaver bird** lives in Africa and Asia, and, as you can guess, it weaves quite an intricate nest. The male weaver bird weaves the nest, from grass, to woo his mate. The nest hangs from a tree branch, like a stocking, and its entrance is usually off to the side, making it difficult for predators to get in.

The **termite** is one of millions in a colony, and they work together, using soil, saliva, and mud, to build their mound. Termites build the tallest and most elaborate nests of any animal. A termite mound can be 6.1 meters (20 feet) tall and can last for years.

It's very dry in the southern Sahara Desert of Africa, where the **desert crocodile** lives – a place that can go six to eight months without rain! During these times, when there is little water to be found, the crocodile makes a burrow, where it sinks into a deep sleep, without eating. Although the desert crocodile estivates to escape the worst of the heat, sometimes it will crawl out of its burrow to lie on the rocks for fresh air.

© W. Allan Hancock

17

MIGRATION & NAVIGATION

Some animals travel thousands of miles for reasons linked to seasonal change, climate, and the availability of food. Scientists know much about why animals migrate, but how they instinctually navigate the skies, land, and seas remains a mystery.

Each fall, about 30,000 **red-sided garter snakes** gather from all over the Province of Manitoba, Canada, to hibernate in communal pits around the province's Interlake area. In the spring, when the weather warms, the snakes slither back to their own homes.

© W. Allan Hancock

Salmon are born in freshwater creeks, but soon after, they swim out to the salty sea, where they live for seven years. After that, salmon make their way back, across thousands of miles, to spawn in the very same creek that they were born in.

Found along the Arctic coast, **bar-tailed godwits** are shorebirds that make the longest nonstop migratory flight in the world. They've flown all the way from Alaska to New Zealand without stopping once! That's 11,500 kilometers (7,146 miles)!

Before the North American **predaceous diving beetle** leaps into the water for prey, it sucks in an air bubble with its spiracles (which it uses the way a scuba diver uses an air tank). Once the beetle hits the water surface, it propels itself by using its hind legs as flippers.

Bats use echolocation to navigate in the dark. Their high-pitched screams create sound waves that travel through the air, bouncing off any object: an insect to eat or a tree to avoid. The echoes that bounce back tell bats where the objects are, how big they are, and how far away they are.

DIET

Many genetic and environmental factors determine what, when, and how an animal eats.

Found in Cuba, the **bee hummingbird** is the smallest bird in the world – it weighs less than a penny! It needs a lot of energy to beat its wings up to eighty times per second, so it consumes a lot of calories. When hungry, the bee hummingbird laps up nectar from flowers. It eats half its total body mass and drinks eight times its body weight in water each day!

The **caribou**'s diet consists of mainly lichen, a plant material high in carbohydrates. Since it lives in the Arctic, it's important for the caribou to stay warm. Special microorganisms in its stomach allow it to digest the lichen, which generates the caribou's body heat and provides a kind of "antifreeze" that helps it survive in -60ºC (-76ºF) temperatures.

© W. Allan Hancock.

The **giant tortoise** is found in the Galapagos Islands. It eats a lot of food that wouldn't appeal to many other animals. One of the giant tortoise's favorite meals is the leaves of the prickly pear cactus.

Although the **silkworm** was originally native to northern China, it is now bred all over the world. It eats one thing only: toxic mulberry leaves. The silkworm has a special enzyme in its digestive system that allows it to eat poisonous mulberry leaves without getting sick.

© W. Allan Hancock

The **parrot fish** has a large set of teeth that grows continuously, and it uses them to scrape algae off coral reefs. This keeps the reefs healthy, but it also means that the ground-up coral leaves the fish's body as deposits of white sand – helping to build those gorgeous beaches that we all like to lie on!

You'll find the **coconut crab** on tropical islands along the Pacific and Indian oceans. The coconut crab is a land-dweller, and it is gigantic: It can measure half a meter (1.6 feet) from claw to claw! The crab uses its powerful pincers to open the tough shells of fallen coconuts.

HUNTING

Whether it's grazing, rooting, or filter feeding, each species finds food in its own particular way. For animals, successfully finding food means survival and healthy offspring.

The **peregrine falcon**, found around the world, will dive from great heights for its prey. Folding its wings to its sides and using its "goggles," clear membranes that protect its eyes, the falcon swoops down at speeds of up to 320 kilometers (199 miles) per hour. It is the fastest animal on Earth! Keeping its talons extended, the falcon strikes its prey with a forceful impact.

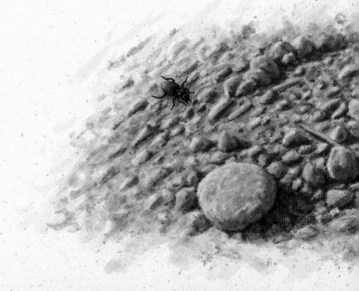

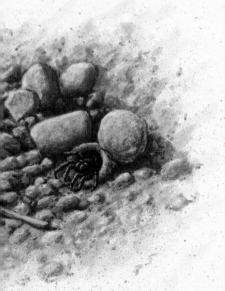

The **cheetah** dines on fast food: gazelle, springbok, and impala. That means the cheetah has to be quicker than its prey. Found in Africa and southwestern Asia, the cheetah is the fastest land mammal. It can go from 0 to 112 kilometers (70 miles) per hour in two seconds – that's as swift as a Formula One race car! A cheetah's claws provide traction, and its tail moves like a rudder, allowing it to make unexpected sharp turns.

Native to many places around the world, the **trap-door spider** has an ingenious way of hunting. It lives in a burrow with a trapdoor made from silk and soil. It waits for its prey on the other side of the door, and when an unsuspecting insect nears its trap, the spider will open the door, leap out, and capture its prey, dragging it into its burrow.

© W. Allan Hancock

The eight arms of an **octopus** are lined with strong suction cups that help it firmly hold its prey. The mouth of an octopus looks like a parrot's beak, and it has a toothed tongue to drill holes in stuff, for instance, a crab's shell. The octopus injects its prey with a toxin before devouring it. It may look harmless, but the octopus has been known to kill small sharks!

Like a living battery, the **electric eel** has three different organs that generate electricity. It has poor eyesight, so it emits low-level charges as radar to detect prey. This freshwater fish can discharge electricity simultaneously from each organ to stun its prey, delivering jolts of up to 600 volts!

DEFENSE

Animals rely on their natural defenses, and many have developed amazing tactics to protect themselves from predators: from camouflage to using strength, speed, and trickery.

Found mostly in North, South, and Central America, the **skunk** growls and stamps the ground when it feels threatened. If that doesn't help, as a last measure, it will lift its tail, turn its backside toward the danger, and spray a foul-smelling musk. The skunk can squirt its musk as far as 6 meters (20 feet), and you can smell it a kilometer away!

The **willow ptarmigan** is from the Arctic regions so it changes its plumage three times a year. In winter, it is as white as the snow. But once the snow melts, it molts into a brownish, blackish color to blend in with the rocky, muddy background. By summer, it is completely brown.

Four-eyed butterfly fish are found in tropical reefs around the world. With a large, dark spot on both sides of their tails, the bottom ends of a butterfly fish are often mistaken for their heads by predators. When they are attacked from behind, these fish have enough time to make their escape!

The **cuttlefish** is possibly the weirdest looking animal on Earth, but it's also one of the most unique. Found in tropical oceans, it's actually not a fish; it's a mollusk. Special skin cells (papillae) allow the cuttlefish to change color and texture to match its surroundings. It can be smooth and speckled like rocks or spiky and white as coral reefs. The cuttlefish can go completely unseen, keeping it safe from predators!

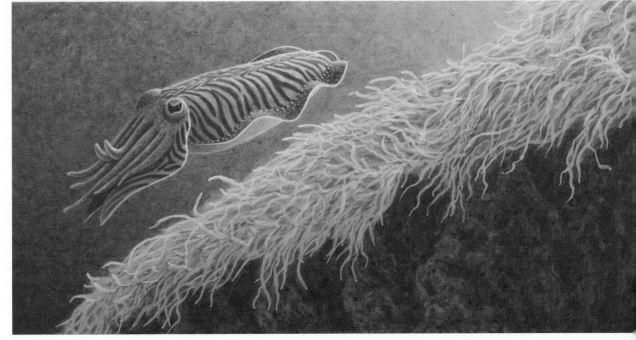

Found in the tropics, the **iguana lizard** can drop its tail to escape its predators. And after a snakebite, the iguana can drop its tail before the poison spreads to the rest of its body. It's a handy trick, but one the lizard uses only when it's in danger.

The South American **strawberry poison dart frog** may look like a tasty snack hopping around the rainforest, but it has a not-so-tasty secret: it's poisonous. The strawberry poison dart frog stores tiny portions of toxins in its skin from the plants and insects that it eats, building up a mighty arsenal. Its only natural predator is a snake named *leimadophis epinephelus*, which has built up a resistance to the frog's poison.

Found all over the world, the Asian **swallowtail butterfly** is a gorgeous black-and-yellow color, but as a caterpillar, it starts out the exact shape and color of bird dropping! It's a tough life, but looking like something no bird wants to eat keeps it safe until it's large enough to turn green and hide among the leaves and grass.

ACKNOWLEDGMENTS

Special thanks to Ron Chamney and to my editor, Lauren Bailey, for corralling my facts and herding my sentences! *Margriet*

A sincere thank-you to Grant Kernan at AK Photos, Larry Hanlon and the staff at Peninsula Gallery, Greg Pedersen and Lindsay Branson, and to Mom, Pam, and Aline for the extra childcare! *Allan*

GLOSSARY

Antifreeze: A substance that prevents liquid from freezing.

Bioluminescence: The ability of a living organism to produce light.

Carbohydrates: Food nutrients that provide a source of energy to animals or plants.

Echolocation: A process used to determine the location of an object by the amount of time it takes for an echo to return from the object.

Embryo: The first stage of an animal's development before birth.

Estivation: A state of deep sleep that an animal uses to escape extreme hot or dry weather. During this time, the animal's body temperature drops and its breathing slows.

Hibernation: A state of deep sleep that an animal uses to escape extreme cold weather. During this time, the animal's body temperature drops and its breathing slows.

Joey: A baby marsupial.

Marsupials: Animals that give birth to an undeveloped baby, which continues to mature inside its mother's pouch.

Microorganisms: Microscopic organisms that help animals digest organic (natural) material.

Molt: The shedding of fur, hair, or feathers in order to grow new ones.

Ovoviviparous: Producing live offspring that hatch from an egg inside of the body.

Spiracles: Small breathing holes.

Swim bladder: An oxygen-filled bag inside the body of a fish that allows it to float.

Symbiotic: A relationship between two living things in which each party needs the other to survive.